Yorks
Coast & Moors

John Potter

MYRIAD

LONDON

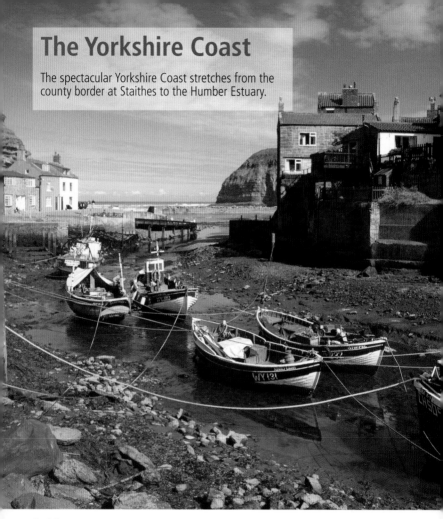

The Yorkshire Coast

The spectacular Yorkshire Coast stretches from the county border at Staithes to the Humber Estuary.

Staithes Known colloquially as "Steers", meaning "landing place", Staithes has a dramatic setting on this rugged stretch of coast north of Whitby. Pretty, white painted cottages are haphazardly perched on any available space and the place oozes charm and history. The sheltered harbour, above and right, is reached from the cobbled main street at the bottom of the steep hill that winds down from the busy Whitby to Loftus road. Captain Cook received his first taste of the sea and ships at Staithes, which has long been a honeypot for writers and artists.

Runswick Bay Just above Runswick Bay's long sandy beach stands the boat park with its many *cobles* (small wooden fishing boats). The village has a tiny Methodist chapel, an Institute – a local meeting place which was opened in 1870 – an old lifeboat house and a former coastguard house with a thatched roof. Runswick has suffered many times from the ravages of the North Sea and in 1682 a landslide destroyed the entire village with the exception of one cottage. Miraculously, no villagers were hurt.

Sandsend This pretty little fishing village is located at the foot of Lythe Bank where the sandy beach that begins at Whitby, just two miles to the south, comes to an abrupt end. There are many picturesque stone cottages set against a backdrop of cliffs and beside two meandering streams which flow out onto the long sandy beach. Sandsend has some of the best surf on this stretch of the coast and has a reputation as a local surfers' paradise. These hardy individuals are often to be seen in all weathers enjoying the huge waves.
If you follow some of the pleasant local walks you will discover the trackbed of the disused coastal railway and the earthworks of Mulgrave Castle hidden away in Mulgrave Woods, just inland. Sandsend was once important for the mining of alum; the waste on Sandsend Ness is the result of more than 250 years of quarrying which ended in the middle of the 19th century.

The Jurassic coast The stretch of coastline between Staithes and Port Mulgrave is one of the most famous Jurassic sites in northern England. Ammonite specimens and the remains of dinosaurs and other reptiles can be found on the foreshore; the best time to look is following storms. But beachcombers and fossil-hunters should always take care to check the tide times before setting off on an expedition. The beach at Kettleness (below) is a magnet for fossil-hunters who benefit from a regular supply of specimens.

Whitby Often referred to as "Captain Cook's Country", the seaside town of Whitby and the surrounding countryside, from where the young James Cook drew his inspiration, is steeped in maritime history. Cook was born in Marton, a small village just south of Middlesbrough. His first job was in Staithes, where he assisted the merchant William Sanderson. In 1746 he took up residence in John Walker's house, an elegant 17th-century harbourside house in Grape Lane, where he served his apprenticeship and learned about navigation and seamanship. It is now the splendid Captain Cook Memorial Museum; together with exhibits on the life and times of Cook it also houses important maritime paintings and has an exhibition on Whitby past and present.

9

Saltwick Bay One mile south-east of Whitby, the low rocky outcrop of Saltwick Nab lies at the southern end of Saltwick Bay. On either side of this beach are vast rock platforms which are only revealed as the tide recedes.

Robin Hood's Bay Picturesque and full of character, the fishing village of Robin Hood's Bay is a maze of steep winding streets and cobbled ginnels (narrow alleyways between houses) which are lined with old houses and cottages, many with red pantiled roofs.

Ravenscar Located 183m (600ft) above sea level, Ravenscar is one of the wildest and most exposed places in Yorkshire. The winds that blow across the North Sea sweep down from the Arctic Ocean, so it's no surprise that the once planned town (a resort to rival nearby Scarborough) fell into difficulties and was not finally developed here.

Scarborough The ruined Norman castle and its headland which stands 150ft (46m) above the harbour, dominate Scarborough's skyline. On a clear day a fantastic view can be enjoyed from Oliver's Mount, high above the town. Scarborough's Spa Complex, with its superb parks, gardens, theatres and conference hall, sits majestically beside the principal bathing beach. Scarborough became a major fishing port after King Henry II built the castle in the 1170s and this led to the development of the famous Scarborough Fair, a six-week trading festival, which attracted merchants from all over Europe.

Bempton At 400ft (122m), Bempton, situated just north of Flamborough Head, has some of the highest cliffs on the east coast of Britain, and is famous as a seabird reserve, featuring the only gannet colony in mainland Britain. Access for visitors is easy by car or on foot, from the village of Bempton one mile inland. Gannets can be seen at Bempton between January and November and are most active between April and August. The Bempton RSPB visitor centre is open daily throughout the year.

Flamborough The coastline at Flamborough is magnificent: Thornwick Bay (above) is just one of the many sheltered shingle coves fronting the sea, and many have sea caves and dramatic stacks. The cliffs and coves teem with seabirds. A lighthouse was first built at Flamborough in 1669 by Sir John Clayton, but it was never kindled. The present lighthouse was built by John Matson of Bridlington in 1806 at a cost of £8,000. There are two schools of thought as to the origins of the place name. In the Domesday book this part of the coastline is called "Flaneberg", from the Saxon word *flaen* meaning dart – a possible reference to the shape of the headland. Alternatively, the name could be derived from "the place of the flame".

Sewerby The village of Sewerby is a tiny hamlet on the coast just two miles north of Bridlington. Sewerby Hall is set in 50 acres of landscaped gardens and is a Grade 1 listed building. The house was built between 1714 and 1720 by John Greame. The rooms on the ground floor are in Georgian, Regency and Victorian styles. The beach at Sewerby (below), with Bridlington in the distance, is constantly being eroded.

Bridlington The bustling town of Bridlington has all the essential ingredients for the perfect holiday resort. There are two glorious long sandy beaches, miles of elegant promenades, a pretty harbour, together with arcades, shops, amusements, restaurants and cafés. Flamborough Head and the lighthouse are clearly visible from the north pier and beach. In recent years the large fleet of trawlers has diminished and now the harbour buzzes with the sound of yachts, private fishing boats, pleasurecraft and the popular *Yorkshire Belle*, which offers sea tours up and down the coast.

Hornsea This small seaside resort is situated 16 miles (26km) north of Hull and 14 miles (22km) south of Bridlington. Some of the houses in the historic town centre date back to the 15th century. One of Hornsea's best known attractions is its Mere – the largest freshwater lake in Yorkshire.

Spurn Point Situated on the north bank of the entrance to the river Humber, Spurn Point is a beautiful and unique place. The three-mile long finger of land that snakes out into the Humber estuary is constantly being reshaped by coastal erosion. This is a very important location for shipping in the area as it is the home of the Humber lighthouse. Spurn Bird Observatory was opened to visitors in 1946 and since then has provided birdwatchers with an ideal location from which to observe spring and autumn migration.

Withernsea The lighthouse at Withernsea stands in the middle of the town showing that, even as far back as the 1800s, there were worries about coastal erosion. Climb the 144 steps to the lamp room and there are breathtaking views of the town and countryside. The base of the lighthouse has both RNLI and HM Coastguard exhibits. There is also a local history room with Victorian and Edwardian photographs including the railway and pier.

Humber Bridge This elegant and dramatic structure was built to link the communities of north Lincolnshire and Humberside. The north tower of this beautiful suspension bridge is sited on the high-water line and the south tower founded in shallow water 1,650ft (500m) from the shore. It is an amazing example of engineering and was developed from a design originally used for the Severn Bridge.

Hull Marina The Hull marina complex was constructed in 1983 and occupies the site of the former Humber and Railway docks. Located in the heart of the city, today the marina is a haven for sailing craft and yachts of all types and provides over 250 permanent berths. The large black boat is the old Spurn Light Boat.

The Deep The gleaming glass and aluminium marine life centre called The Deep opened in 2002. Designed by architect Sir Terry Farrell it stands at the confluence of the rivers Hull and Humber and is part of the vision of regeneration for the city of Hull. It was conceived to entertain and educate its visitors about the world's oceans.

The North York Moors

The landscape of this dramatic area which borders the Yorkshire Heritage Coast is a blend of wild and beautiful moorland interspersed with pretty villages and market towns.

Roseberry Topping Bordering the North York Moors and Cleveland, the distinctive half-cone shape of Roseberry Topping dominates much of the countryside around Guisborough. The hill's peculiar shape is due to the fact that half the summit has collapsed, as the result of either a geological fault or the presence of many old alum and ironstone mines near the top. Close by stands a monument to James Cook who was born in nearby Marton.

Danby Dale This wild corner of the Moors consists of two secluded valleys, Great and Little Fryup, made up of a scattering of farms and cottages. Winding off the Esk Valley the area is totally unspoilt and surrounded by magnificent purple heather-clad moors with trails and walks across the moorland.

Grouse butts The high moorland here is dotted with distinctive circular stone structures which can sometimes be mistaken for ancient cairns or early houses. They are, in fact, grouse butts which are used to give cover on open moorland for gamekeepers and shooters during the grouse season. Grouse butts are usually spread in a long line and at a considerable distance apart to reduce the risk of accidents.

Castleton Situated in the upper Esk Valley, the linear village of Castleton sits proudly on a high ridge, where the lush green secluded valleys of Westerdale and Danby Dale come together on the northern fringe of the North York Moors. In summer the Castleton Show draws huge crowds to see the show jumping and the road race. This distant view of the village in winter (right), was taken from Castleton Rigg.

Westerdale, Bilsdale and Blakey Ridge Some of the finest high moorland walks in northern England traverse these hills. A 24-mile section of the famous coast-to-coast trail from St Bees in Cumbria to Robin Hood's Bay crosses Blakey Ridge from Claybank, largely along remote and uninhabited moorland. The 41-mile Lyke Wake Walk is close by. The Old Sun Inn, also known as the Spout House, is at Bilsdale.

Falling Foss waterfall Located close to the tiny hamlet of Little Beck on a tributary of the river Esk, this beautiful waterfall can be reached via a pleasant woodland walk through Little Beck and May Beck Wood.

Mallyan Spout is the highest waterfall on the North Yorks Moors. It tumbles 60ft (18m) down the deep and beautiful West Beck Gorge (left) close to the Mallyan Spout Hotel at the western edge of the village of Goathland – a favourite village with visitors who come to take a ride on a steam train on the North York Moors Railway.

Rosedale Rosedale is a long extended valley located in the heart of the North York Moors. It stretches out in a south-easterly direction from Westerdale Moor and Danby High Moor towards Hartoft End and Cropton Forest. The river Seven flows throughout its length gathering water from the numerous moorland springs and streams. The railbed of the disused Rosedale Mineral Railway is clearly visible around the perimeter of the dale and stunning views of the valley can be enjoyed from many of the moorland paths and in particular from Chimney Bank Top.

Blakey Ridge The wild moorland of Blakey Ridge is peppered with Bronze Age standing stones and burial mounds. The views from here across both Rosedale to the east and Farndale to the west are quite simply breathtaking, particularly after heavy snow. The remote 16th century Lion Inn is a tourist honeypot, where real ales, a cosy atmosphere and good food can always be guaranteed. It is sited at the highest point of the Yorkshire Moors National Park. Each year in July the Lion Inn music festival draws thousands of visitors to this stunning setting to enjoy the event where live bands and musicians perform on stage in the pub car park.

Grosmont A steam train arrives at Grosmont station, the northern terminus of the much-loved North York Moors Railway. Situated in the heart of the Esk Valley, Grosmont was originally Grandimont, which takes its name from a small priory founded around 1200. The priory once stood near the north bank of the river Esk but sadly there are no remains of this ancient building to be seen today.

Hutton-le-Hole One of the most popular stopping-off points for visitors to the North York Moors, Hutton's broad village green, which looks down on Hutton Beck and is dotted with moorland sheep, makes an ideal spot for a summer picnic. After a dusting of light snow in early spring, the village green with its row of terraced houses make this a picture-postcard scene. The Ryedale Folk Museum, Yorkshire's leading open-air museum, has historic buildings depicting the daily life of North Yorkshire people from the earliest inhabitants up to the 1950s.

Stone markers This dramatic standing stone is located near the road that links Hutton-Le-Hole to Castleton. The area around Blakey Ridge and Westerdale is scattered with dramatic Bronze Age mounds and standing stones.

Bransdale Only accessible via two small moorland roads, Bransdale is one of the North York Moors best-kept secrets. Running north to south, between Farndale and Bilsdale, and approximately 7 miles (12km) north of Helmsley, it is a jewel of a dale, consisting of a few scattered farmsteads and cottages set in glorious scenery. Hodge Beck runs through the length of the dale and then, at the southern end, runs out through a narrow-sided valley into Sleightholme Dale and then into Kirkdale.

Rievaulx Abbey Traditionally Cistercian abbeys were built on an east-west axis, but because of the steep slope at Rievaulx a north-south alignment was adopted. Like all Cistercian houses the location was deliberately secluded from the outside world and this particular site in the depths of the narrow river Rye valley must have provided the monks with a haven of peace and solitude. The 13th-century church is reputed to have been one of the finest monastic churches in northern Britain and thankfully remains substantially intact. The abbey site is now owned and run by English Heritage, whereas Rievaulx Terrace and Temples (right), situated on an escarpment above the abbey, is owned by the National Trust.

Helmsley Located on the Thirsk to Scarborough road, Helmsley is one of the prettiest towns in north Yorkshire. A pretty stream runs through the town at the back of the market square (below) complete with a stone arch bridge. The poet William Wordsworth stayed at the Black Swan Inn in the centre of the town when courting Mary, his future wife. Helmsley Castle (left) is a spectacular ruin and once guarded the Rye Valley. The early 13th-century castle is surrounded by a formidable double ditch cut from solid rock.

The Cleveland Way The Cleveland Way long-distance footpath starts in the market town of Helmsley and traverses the upland ridge on the edge of the North York Moors before reaching the coast at Saltburn by Sea. It then continues along the Yorkshire Heritage Coast and ends at Filey – a distance of 110 miles (177km). The footpath is really two walks in one, the first a walk along high moorland while the second is a walk along one of the most outstanding sections of coastline in Britain. It gives excellent views of Lake Gormire from Sutton Bank (below).

White Horse Kilburn Just beyond Roulston Scar lies the well-known landmark the White Horse of Kilburn, built by local teacher John Hodgson and his pupils in 1857. The White Horse, which is visible throughout large parts of the Vale of York, was intended to resemble the hill figures which are cut into the chalk downs in many parts of southern England. However, Sutton Bank is not made from chalk, so the outline has to be artificially whitened at regular intervals using limestone chips. The best view of the horse is reported to be from two elevated benches just inside the northern boundary of Kilburn village.

Kirkbymoorside The market town of Kirkbymoorside is considered by many to be the gateway to the North York Moors. A sizeable town situated on the busy A170 Helmsley to Pickering road, market day is Wednesday when traders from the area come together to sell their goods. It has a wide variety of shops and services and yet enjoys a tranquil atmosphere helped by the fine ornate Yorkshire stone buildings that line the main street. Locals call the town "Kirby" and are for-

tunate to live in a town with such an appealing aspect, surrounded by green rolling hills. All Saints church (below) is set back from the main street, and photographed here from a recently landscaped area on the edge of town. Manor Vale Woodland is an ancient woodland that was bought by the council in 1993; it is now actively managed for wildlife and recreation.

Gillamoor The pretty village of Gillamoor lies 2.5 miles (4km) north of Kirkbymoorside on the minor road that links Fadmoor to Hutton-Le-Hole. The village is famously known for its Surprise View (left) at the eastern end of the hamlet, beside St Aidan's church. This part of lower Farndale is often known as "daffodil dale" due to the swathes of these attractive flowers which adorn the local hedgerows and cover the river banks in spring. The tiny Church of St Aidans (below) was rebuilt single-handedly by James Smith of Farndale in 1802 using stone from the dismantled medieval church in Bransdale. The church has a simple but beautiful interior largely constructed from wood.

Farndale The tiny and picturesque hamlet of Church Houses (above and below) nestles between the mighty Rudland Rigg and Blakey Ridge in glorious scenery at the heart of this much-loved dale. Perhaps best known for its wild daffodils in spring, Farndale attracts up to 40,000 visitors each April. The daffodil walk follows the valley bottom beside the river Dove, from Low Mill to Church Houses and the welcoming Feversham Arms.

Hole of Horcum This unusual feature is a huge natural amphitheatre hollowed out of the heather-clad moor situated beside the A169 Pickering to Whitby road. Legend has it that "The Devil's Punchbowl", as it is known locally, was made by a giant named Wade who scooped out the rocks and earth, tossing them two miles east to Blakey Topping.

Sinnington Situated in Ryedale midway between Kirkbymoorside and Pickering, this attractive village on the banks of the river Seven was once a stop on the Gilling and Pickering railway line which opened in 1875. There is a circular walk along the banks of the Seven, to All Saints church and then back through Mill Wood, and Hob Banks Wood both spectacular in spring when the daffodils are in bloom.

Lastingham This peaceful village is best known for the magnificent Crypt Church of St Mary. It was built around 1078 as a shrine to the monks Cedd and Chad who founded a Celtic monastery on this site four centuries earlier. The crypt is thought to be the only one in England to have an apse (rounded end) together with a chancel, nave and side aisles. Over the centuries the crypt became a place of pilgrimage and thousands of Christians would make the journey over Lastingham Moor to visit the burial spot of Cedd who, with his brother Chad, hailed from Lindisfarne in Northumbria.

Levisham The picturesque village of Levisham is located in the heart of the North York Moors National Park and is an attractive stop on the North York Moors Railway. The village nestles above the quiet and winding wooded valley of Newton Dale, seven miles north of Pickering. The small church of St John the Baptist (below) lies at the top of the village where the road and a footpath, which meanders across woods and fields, leads to the railway station in the bottom of the valley. Levisham station is set in the secluded and scenic Newton Dale Valley. Newton Dale Hall is a walker's request stop on the steam train and a starting point for many lovely walks. The station has been used as the location for a range of television programmes and feature films including *All Creatures Great and Small*, *Poirot*, *Sherlock Holmes* and *Brideshead Revisited*.

Hackness This quiet and beautiful village was first mentioned in the Ecclesiastical History of the English People written by the Venerable Bede in the early eighth century. Bede described how Saint Hilda, abbess of Whitby and an active figure in the early English church, founded a nunnery in Hackness in 680AD, the year of her death. St Peter's Church (above) houses a priceless Anglo-Saxon cross, a fine example of Anglo-Saxon Northumbrian sculpture.

Pickering The elegant market town of Pickering can trace its history back to the 3rd century BC. It has a motte-and-bailey castle with Norman remnants. In the centre of the town is Beck Isle Museum of Rural Life. The museum has 27 galleries and visitors are transported back through time as they pass through a wide variety of recreated settings including a cobblers' shop, blacksmiths, chemists' shop, dairy and village store. Of particular interest is the gallery which features the work of local photographer Sydney Smith who captured rural life in and around Pickering in the early 20th century. With his themes of village events and working lives, he is thought of as a successor to Frank Meadow Sutcliffe of Whitby.

Thornton-le-Dale This pretty village lies to the east of Pickering on the A170 Scarborough road. In the centre of the town close to the crossroads is a small green, a market cross and stocks. The village has gift shops, tea rooms and the pretty Trench pond near the main car park; alongside the roads to Malton and Scarborough a shimmering stream tumbles over a bed of cobbles. The 17th century thatched Beck Isle cottage lies along the high street in the direction of the bridge. All Saints church dates from the 14th century and Sir Richard Cholmeley, known as The Black Knight of the North, is buried in the chancel. The Thornton-le-Dale Show is held at The Showground each August.

The Cleveland Way This photograph was taken at Whitestone Cliff on the Cleveland Way long-distance footpath, looking north towards the village of Boltby. On the right is the dramatic view from the Cleveland Way on Sutton Bank looking across the Vale of York.